Mastering Google Gemini

Unlock the Full Power of Google's AI to Automate Tasks, Create Content, Boost Productivity, and Stay Organized in Daily Life

MILA ASHFORD

1

TABLE OF CONTENTS

Introduction

In a world where technology is evolving faster than we can comprehend, artificial intelligence has become the cornerstone of transformation. Imagine having a digital assistant so powerful, so intuitive, that it could seamlessly integrate into every aspect of your life—personal and professional. Welcome to Google Gemini—the future of AI, right at your fingertips.

But don't be fooled into thinking this is just another chatbot. Google Gemini isn't merely a tool that answers questions or chats with you when you need it. This is a revolutionary AI assistant that understands the depth of your needs, anticipates your next move, and makes your daily tasks not just manageable but effortlessly efficient. Think of Gemini as a supercharged version of your most helpful assistant, constantly learning, adapting, and evolving to offer a more intelligent, personalized experience.

So, why is Gemini more than just a chatbot? The answer lies in its intelligence and versatility. Unlike traditional AI models, which simply respond based on programmed data, Gemini works alongside you—enhancing productivity, boosting creativity, and organizing your day-to-day tasks like never before. Whether you're scheduling meetings, drafting emails, brainstorming ideas, or even planning vacations, Gemini has the power to make your life simpler, smarter, and more connected.

AI's Role in Productivity, Content Creation, and Organization

Artificial intelligence is no longer a distant concept confined to sci-fi movies. It's here, revolutionizing how we work, create, and organize. From managing complex workflows to generating compelling content at the click of a button, AI is transforming every corner of our lives. But for all its capabilities, the true potential of AI lies in its ability to enhance human productivity. Google Gemini doesn't just automate; it amplifies. Whether you're a student, professional, entrepreneur, or content creator, Gemini helps you maximize efficiency and creativity like never before.

In the world of content creation, AI-powered tools like Gemini are game-changers. Writers, marketers, and business owners are now empowered to produce high-quality content in a fraction of the time it used to take. By automating routine tasks and providing on-demand suggestions, Gemini enables you to focus on what truly matters—bringing your ideas to life. For organization, Gemini acts as an intelligent assistant that helps you juggle multiple tasks with ease, whether it's managing schedules, creating to-do lists, or organizing your thoughts into structured, actionable plans.

What This Book Will Help You Achieve

This book is your roadmap to mastering Google Gemini and harnessing its full potential. As you embark on this journey, you'll not only learn how to use Gemini effectively, but you'll unlock its hidden capabilities—those that go beyond the surface and into the realm of true AI-powered efficiency. By the end of this guide, you'll understand how to integrate Gemini seamlessly into your daily routines, supercharge your productivity, and create content that stands out.

More than just learning the "how," this book will show you why Gemini should become an indispensable tool in your life. You'll discover how this AI assistant can take over repetitive tasks, streamline your workflow, and free up more time for what really matters. Whether you're looking to automate your home, boost your business, or supercharge your personal projects, the possibilities with Google Gemini are endless.

Prepare yourself to dive into the transformative world of AI, where your productivity, creativity, and organization will reach new heights. Google Gemini isn't just a tool—it's the future of artificial intelligence, and it's waiting for you to unlock its full potential.

Chapter 1

Understanding Google Gemini

The Evolution from Bard to Gemini

When Google first introduced **Bard**, it set the stage for a new wave of AI-driven conversation models. Bard was a step into the future, enabling users to interact with an intelligent system that could generate responses based on vast amounts of data. However, as powerful as Bard was, it didn't quite meet the evolving needs of users seeking a more intuitive, capable, and versatile AI assistant. Enter **Google**

Gemini—the next-generation AI that goes far beyond its predecessor.

Gemini isn't just an upgrade from Bard; it's a complete transformation. The leap from Bard to Gemini marks a significant shift in Google's approach to artificial intelligence. While Bard was mainly focused on offering quick responses and handling general inquiries, Gemini was designed with a deeper understanding of context, complexity, and personalized assistance. Google has combined its powerful AI models, integrating advanced natural language processing and machine learning to create an AI that understands not just what you ask, but **why** you're asking it.

Gemini's capabilities are built on years of refinement and user feedback, culminating in an AI that can handle more complex queries, offer more nuanced suggestions, and provide real-time assistance across a broader range of tasks. The AI has evolved from a tool that simply answers questions to an intelligent companion that adapts to your lifestyle, boosts your productivity, and assists with creative endeavors.

Gemini's Position in the AI Landscape

In the vast landscape of artificial intelligence, **Google Gemini** stands out among the competition. When comparing Gemini to other well-known models like **ChatGPT** from OpenAI and **Claude** from Anthropic, the unique strength of Gemini lies in its

integration with Google's suite of products and services.

Whereas **ChatGPT** is praised for its conversational abilities and general-purpose AI model, Gemini takes things a step further by blending this conversational prowess with seamless access to Google's ecosystem—products like Gmail, Google Docs, YouTube, Google Calendar, and more. While ChatGPT offers incredible results for general queries and content creation, Gemini elevates productivity, organization, and task management by working as part of a larger, cohesive system.

Moreover, **Claude** by Anthropic brings its focus on ethical AI and safety, but it doesn't yet match the ecosystem-wide integration that Gemini offers. Gemini is more than just an AI assistant—it's a **connector** that brings together all the tools and platforms that you already use on a daily basis.

In short, while models like ChatGPT and Claude offer impressive capabilities, **Google Gemini** holds a unique position by deeply integrating into the Google ecosystem, making it more than just another AI tool. It's an intelligent assistant, a productivity booster, and a content generator that learns from and adapts to your preferences across devices and platforms.

Key Features and Capabilities of Google Gemini

Google Gemini stands out for its **advanced capabilities** that empower users to complete tasks faster and more effectively.

Unlike traditional AI, which can only respond based on pre-programmed knowledge, Gemini is built to **understand context**, anticipate your needs, and execute complex actions based on your goals. Here are some of its key features:

1. **Contextual Understanding**: Gemini can remember and learn from previous interactions, allowing it to respond more accurately to ongoing projects and tasks. Whether you're revisiting a document or continuing a conversation from a week ago, Gemini adapts its responses based on your prior engagements.

2. **Multimodal Abilities**: Beyond text, Gemini excels in handling different

types of media. It understands images, audio, and video, making it a truly multimodal assistant. You can ask it to interpret images, transcribe audio files, or even generate video content ideas.

3. **Real-Time Assistance**: Gemini provides real-time support as you work across Google tools like Docs, Sheets, and Slides. It can suggest edits, generate content, summarize information, and even automate tasks such as scheduling or creating reports.

4. **Personalized Experience**: Over time, Gemini learns from your habits and preferences. Whether you're organizing your calendar, composing

an email, or brainstorming a new project, Gemini personalizes its suggestions to fit your style and needs, becoming a more effective assistant as you use it.

5. **Collaboration with Google Workspace**: One of the standout features of Gemini is how it integrates seamlessly with Google's suite of products. From drafting emails in Gmail to building presentations in Google Slides, Gemini is there to enhance your workflow.

Differences Between Gemini 1.0 and Gemini 1.5

As with most evolving technologies, **Google Gemini** has seen updates and improvements over time. The **transition from Gemini 1.0 to Gemini 1.5** marked an important development in the AI's capabilities. While Gemini 1.0 was a powerful tool, the improvements in **Gemini 1.5** took it to new heights.

1. **Enhanced Understanding**: Gemini 1.5 has a deeper comprehension of context, meaning it can handle more complex queries and provide better suggestions. It's smarter at anticipating the needs of users, offering proactive solutions rather than simply reacting to requests.

2. **Faster Response Times**: With an upgraded backend architecture, Gemini 1.5 is faster at processing requests. This improvement is especially important for users working on time-sensitive projects, where speed and efficiency are crucial.

3. **Broader Integration**: While Gemini 1.0 worked well within the Google ecosystem, Gemini 1.5 brings **even deeper integration** with external platforms, allowing users to interact with other tools beyond Google's services. Whether it's syncing with third-party apps or providing cross-platform recommendations, Gemini 1.5 extends its utility.

4. **Refined Multimodal Features**:
   Gemini 1.5 enhances its ability to work with multimedia, offering more accurate and diverse responses when handling images, videos, and audio. This makes it an even more powerful tool for creators, marketers, and professionals.

5. **Improved Ethical AI Features**:
   Gemini 1.5 has better safeguards in place to ensure responsible AI use. Google has refined the model to handle sensitive topics with greater care, ensuring more accurate and ethical responses.

How Gemini Integrates with the Google Ecosystem

Google has always been at the forefront of digital tools, from search engines to cloud storage, productivity suites, and beyond. **Gemini's** power lies in its seamless **integration** with these tools, making it an indispensable part of the Google ecosystem.

1. **Google Docs & Sheets**: Gemini assists you in writing, editing, and brainstorming content in **Google Docs**, while also helping you manage data and automate tasks in **Google Sheets**. It can generate reports, summarize information, or even draft entire sections based on your inputs.

2. **Gmail**: Gemini integrates with **Gmail** to help you manage your inbox. It can prioritize emails, generate responses, or even remind you of important follow-ups. You no longer have to dig through your inbox to find essential messages—Gemini keeps you organized and on top of your correspondence.

3. **Google Calendar**: With **Google Calendar** integration, Gemini becomes your personal scheduling assistant, helping you organize meetings, events, and reminders without missing a beat. It can even suggest optimal times for meetings based on your existing schedule.

4. **YouTube and Google Search**: Gemini can help you find relevant content on **YouTube** and perform deep, targeted searches via **Google Search**, providing answers, video suggestions, and even analyzing trends.

By integrating deeply with these tools, **Google Gemini** creates an **interconnected digital experience**, allowing you to move seamlessly between tasks, applications, and devices. Whether you're using your phone, tablet, or desktop, Gemini is there, optimizing your workflow and making sure nothing falls through the cracks.

Chapter 2

Setting Up and Getting Started

Accessing Gemini on Android, iOS, and Web

Google Gemini offers a seamless experience across multiple platforms, including **Android**, **iOS**, and **the web**, ensuring that you can access it anytime, anywhere. Whether you're working from your smartphone, tablet, or desktop, Gemini is designed to integrate smoothly across your devices.

1. **Accessing Gemini on Android and iOS**

   For most users, the easiest way to get started with Gemini is by downloading the **Gemini app** on your mobile device. It is available for both **Android** and **iOS** users.

   - **On Android:** Head to the **Google Play Store** and search for "Google Gemini." Once you find the app, tap **Install**, and it will automatically download to your device. After the installation is complete, open the app, and you will be guided through a simple setup process to get started.

- **On iOS:** The process is similar for iPhone and iPad users. Go to the **App Store**, search for "Google Gemini," and tap **Download**. The app is lightweight and doesn't take long to install. Once it's installed, open it, and you will be prompted to sign in with your Google account.

2. **Accessing Gemini on the Web**
   In addition to the mobile apps, Google Gemini can be accessed through the web. This option is ideal for users who prefer to work from a desktop or laptop. Simply navigate to **gemini.google.com** or access the Gemini app via Google's **Web**

Workspace. There's no need to download anything—just sign in with your Google account, and you're good to go.

Gemini's web version offers the same functionality as its mobile counterparts but is optimized for larger screens, providing a more expansive interface and ease of multitasking. This version is particularly useful for users who want to handle more intensive tasks, such as generating reports, editing documents, or managing email correspondence.

Google Account Requirements and Setup Tips

Before you can fully experience the power of **Google Gemini**, you need a Google account. Luckily, setting up a Google account is quick and straightforward. Here's what you need to know:

1. **Creating a Google Account**
    If you don't already have a Google account, don't worry. Gemini requires an active Google account, but the setup process is simple and free:

    - **Visit** the Google Account creation page at accounts.google.com.

    - **Fill in your details**, including your name, preferred email address, and a secure password.

- ○ **Verify your email address**: Google will send you a verification code to your phone or another email account for additional security.

- ○ **Complete the process** by adding recovery options such as a phone number (optional but recommended for account recovery).

2. **Linking Your Google Account to Gemini**

 After creating your Google account, the next step is to link it with **Gemini**. This is where the integration magic happens. Upon launching the app or visiting the web version of Gemini, you will be prompted to sign in using your Google account credentials.

The process is seamless—simply enter your **Google username** (your Gmail address) and **password**, and you'll be all set. If you've already linked your Google account to other services like Gmail or Google Drive, Gemini will automatically sync with them, making the process faster and easier.

3. **Account Security and Privacy Tips**

Google Gemini handles sensitive information, so it's important to take steps to protect your account. Here are some essential **security tips**:

- ○ **Enable Two-Factor Authentication (2FA)**: This adds an extra layer of security to your Google account. You can enable this via the **Security Settings** of your Google account.

- ○ **Review Permissions**: Regularly review which apps and devices have access to your Google account. This can be done through the **Google Account Settings** under the **Security** tab.

- Use Strong Passwords:
    Always use a unique, complex
    password for your Google
    account to minimize the risk of
    unauthorized access.

Installing and Updating the Gemini App

Keeping your **Gemini app** up-to-date ensures you always have the latest features and security updates. Installing and updating the app is straightforward, but it's important to understand how to manage it on both **Android** and **iOS**.

1. **Installing the Gemini App**

- **On Android:** After downloading Gemini from the Google Play Store, the installation will happen automatically. You simply need to follow the on-screen prompts to complete the setup process.

- **On iOS:** The process is equally simple on iPhones and iPads. After tapping **Download** on the App Store, the app will install automatically, and once it's finished, you can open it to start the setup process.

2. **Updating Gemini**

- **On Android:** You can enable **automatic updates** by going to the Play Store, searching for Gemini, and turning on the automatic update option. Alternatively, you can manually update Gemini by visiting the Play Store, searching for the app, and selecting **Update** when it's available.

- **On iOS:** Open the **App Store**, go to your **Profile**, and scroll down to see available updates. Tap **Update** next to the Gemini app when a new version is available. You can also enable automatic updates in your iOS settings under **App Store**.

Why Updates Matter: Updates often include **bug fixes**, **security patches**, and **new features**. By ensuring that Gemini is up-to-date, you're keeping your experience smooth and free from potential issues. The new features in each update can also introduce enhancements that improve your productivity, such as new integrations or improved usability.

First-Time Walkthrough: Layout, Interface, and Key Functions

Upon launching **Google Gemini** for the first time, you'll be greeted by a clean, minimalist interface designed to help you get straight to work without unnecessary distractions. Here's a detailed walkthrough of the app's layout and the key functions you should familiarize yourself with.

1. **Home Screen Layout**

   The **home screen** of Gemini is divided into several key sections that provide quick access to various tools and services.

   - **Top Navigation Bar**: This contains your profile icon, notification bell, and quick access to settings. You can tap your profile icon to manage your account, and the notification bell will keep you updated with important messages and alerts.

- **Main Dashboard**: The main area of the screen will display your current tasks, documents, and any active projects you are working on. You can easily navigate between your **emails**, **Google Docs**, **Google Drive**, and more, all from this central hub.

- **Sidebar**: On the left side of the screen (in both mobile and web versions), you'll find a collapsible sidebar that gives you quick access to various tools such as **Tasks**, **Notes**, **Search**, and **Quick Links** to Google's other services.

2. **The Sidebar Functions**

   The sidebar is where you'll find the heart of **Google Gemini's** tools, and each section is designed to boost your productivity:

   ○ **Search**: You can quickly search for documents, emails, or tasks across your Google account. This tool also integrates with **Google Search**, so you can search the web without leaving the Gemini app.

   ○ **Tasks**: Create, assign, and manage tasks directly from Gemini. This tool syncs with **Google Calendar** and **Google Keep**, allowing you to set reminders, deadlines, and to-do lists.

- **Notes**: Keep all your notes organized in one place, whether they're handwritten or typed. Gemini's integration with **Google Keep** allows you to sync your notes across all devices.

3. **Key Functions of Gemini**

   Some of the key features of Gemini include:

   - **Contextual Assistant**: Ask Gemini anything, and it will use your history and preferences to provide personalized, relevant answers.

- **Task Automation**: From drafting emails to scheduling appointments, Gemini can automate repetitive tasks to save you time.

- **Multimedia Support**: You can use Gemini to analyze images, transcribe audio, or even generate videos based on your ideas.

- **Integration with Google Workspace**: Gemini integrates deeply with **Google Docs**, **Google Drive**, **Gmail**, and other Google Workspace tools, allowing you to draft content, manage files, and communicate more efficiently.

Linking Gemini with Gmail, Docs, Drive, YouTube, and More

The real power of **Google Gemini** lies in its ability to **integrate with other Google services**, creating a unified digital assistant experience. Here's a closer look at how you can link Gemini to these services:

1. **Linking with Gmail**

   To start, Gemini integrates directly with **Gmail**, offering intelligent assistance for managing your inbox. Gemini can automatically categorize emails, highlight important messages, and even suggest responses. You can link your Gmail by simply signing in to your Google account during the initial setup. Once connected, Gemini will begin optimizing your Gmail usage, from organizing emails into labels to offering quick replies.

2. **Google Docs & Drive**

Gemini helps you write, edit, and organize content within **Google Docs** and **Google Drive**. Once connected, Gemini can create and edit documents, automate formatting, and even suggest improvements. Whether you're writing an email, a report, or a creative piece, Gemini will assist with grammar, tone, and structure.

3. **YouTube Integration**

Gemini isn't just for text-based tasks. It also integrates with **YouTube**, helping you find videos, generate video ideas, or even summarize content. Whether you're a content creator looking for the latest trends or simply trying to find information, Gemini's connection with YouTube makes it a powerful tool for video enthusiasts.

4. **Google Calendar & Keep**

Gemini links seamlessly with **Google Calendar**, allowing it to help you schedule meetings, set reminders, and even find open time slots. Similarly, its integration with **Google Keep** allows you to sync notes and reminders, ensuring that all your ideas and tasks are easily accessible from within Gemini.

Chapter 3

Gemini in Daily Life

In today's fast-paced world, technology has become a vital part of managing our daily lives. We juggle work, personal responsibilities, and leisure activities, all while striving for better efficiency and productivity. Enter **Google Gemini** – a versatile AI tool that aims to make your daily tasks easier, smarter, and more organized.

Using Gemini for Personal Tasks and Organization

Google Gemini offers powerful features that integrate seamlessly into your personal routine. Whether you're managing your day-to-day chores or keeping track of appointments, this AI assistant can help you stay on top of things with minimal effort.

Task Management and Organization

Gemini can assist with managing all aspects of your personal tasks. From simple to-do lists to more complex organization, this AI tool can help create a plan and stick to it. When you feel overwhelmed with everything on your plate, Gemini is just a command away to help you prioritize your day.

For example, you can use Gemini to create lists of tasks such as groceries, errands, or project deadlines. These lists are instantly accessible, so you don't need to worry about keeping track of paper notes or remembering tasks. You can even set recurring tasks that Gemini will automatically remind you about on a daily, weekly, or monthly basis.

Smart Reminders

Gemini's ability to set reminders ensures that you'll never forget important dates or deadlines. Whether it's a simple reminder to take a break or something more substantial, such as a doctor's appointment or an event, Gemini can send you notifications to keep you on track.

You can simply tell Gemini, "Remind me to call Mom at 2 PM tomorrow," and it will send you a reminder at the specified time. Furthermore, if you're someone who relies on location-based reminders, Gemini can remind you of tasks as you approach specific locations, like reminding you to pick up groceries when you're near the store.

Setting Reminders, Making Lists, and Managing Your Day

Efficient time management is one of the cornerstones of productivity, and Google Gemini can help you stay organized throughout the day.

Managing Your Day with Timely Reminders

Imagine having an assistant who not only tracks your calendar but also ensures you never miss a thing. With Gemini, you can set daily agendas and get prompted throughout the day with reminders, helping you stick to your schedule. You can command Gemini to remind you to "start working on the presentation at 9 AM" or "pick up the dry cleaning at 4 PM."

Whether you need a push to begin your morning routine or a nudge to finish a task by the end of the day, Gemini's notifications can help guide you through a productive day.

Creating and Managing Lists

Making lists is a universal technique for staying organized, but maintaining them can sometimes feel like a hassle. Gemini simplifies the process of creating and managing lists. You can use it to set up a variety of lists, such as shopping lists, to-do lists, and even goal lists.

For example, if you're preparing for a trip, you can ask Gemini to create a packing list, adding items as you go along. It will keep everything neatly organized and available for quick access. Need to pick up some items for your home? Just tell Gemini, and it will create a shopping list that's easily updated as you remember new things you need.

You can also use Gemini to set tasks based on your list. If you add "call the dentist" to your to-do list, Gemini can automatically remind you to do it when the time comes, ensuring that important tasks don't get lost in the shuffle.

Summarizing Long Emails, Articles, or YouTube Videos

In our content-heavy world, it's easy to feel overwhelmed by the sheer amount of information we encounter daily. Gemini can help alleviate this problem by summarizing emails, articles, and even video content, saving you time and making sure you absorb only the essential information.

Summarizing Emails

Emails can sometimes become a source of stress, especially when you're dealing with long, intricate threads or lengthy updates. Gemini's summarization capabilities allow you to quickly understand the key points without reading every word.

For instance, if you receive an email with a detailed update on a work project, simply forward it to Gemini and ask it to "Summarize this email for me." Gemini will highlight the most important parts of the message, giving you a concise overview without losing critical information.

Summarizing Articles and News Stories

The internet is full of long articles and blogs, often with more content than we have time to read. With Gemini, you can have articles or news stories summarized in a matter of seconds. Whether it's a technical article or a lifestyle blog post, simply paste the link into Gemini and ask for a brief summary.

This is especially useful when you're trying to keep up with current events but don't have hours to sift through articles. Gemini can quickly provide you with a condensed version, saving you time while ensuring you stay informed.

Summarizing YouTube Videos

Another great feature of Gemini is its ability to summarize YouTube videos. Whether you're watching tutorials, interviews, or product reviews, you can ask Gemini to summarize the key points for you. Simply provide the video link, and Gemini will process it, giving you a breakdown of the main takeaways.

This is a game-changer for anyone who relies on video content but doesn't have the time to sit through the entire length of a video. With Gemini, you get the highlights without the time commitment.

AI Assistance with Travel, Recipes, Shopping, and Planning

Gemini excels in making everyday tasks more manageable, especially when it comes to travel, meal planning, shopping, and organizing events. With a few simple commands, you can streamline various aspects of your daily life.

Travel Assistance

Travel planning can be stressful, but Gemini makes it easier by acting as your personal travel assistant. Whether you're booking a flight, finding a hotel, or planning your itinerary, Gemini can help.

For example, if you're looking for the best flights to a destination, you can ask Gemini, "Find me flights from New York to Paris in June." It will provide options based on your preferences, saving you time that would have otherwise been spent searching multiple websites.

Additionally, Gemini can help you create a travel checklist, remind you of important travel dates, and even offer recommendations on what to do once you arrive at your destination.

Recipe and Meal Planning

If you're someone who struggles with meal planning or need help finding recipes, Gemini can be your go-to assistant in the kitchen. You can ask it to suggest recipes based on ingredients you already have in your pantry. Simply tell Gemini, "I have chicken and broccoli, what can I make?" and it will suggest several recipes you can try.

Gemini can also help with weekly meal planning. If you're trying to eat healthier or stick to a certain diet, Gemini can provide a meal plan that aligns with your dietary goals, including shopping lists for each recipe.

Shopping Assistance

Shopping is another area where Gemini shines. With its ability to generate shopping lists and suggest items, it can take the stress out of making purchases.

For example, if you need to buy a gift for someone, you can ask Gemini, "Suggest a birthday gift for my friend who loves tech gadgets." It will come up with a list of relevant suggestions based on the person's interests. Similarly, for everyday shopping, you can ask Gemini to create a grocery list, and it will add items as you remember them.

Event and Appointment Planning

Gemini also proves invaluable when it comes to planning events and scheduling appointments. Whether you're organizing a family gathering or scheduling meetings for work, Gemini can help you keep everything on track.

You can ask Gemini to assist with finding the best date for an event, reminding you of upcoming appointments, and sending invitations. It can even help you organize the event by suggesting tasks that need to be completed before the event, ensuring that you don't miss any details.

Using Gemini Hands-Free with Voice on Mobile Devices

In a world where multitasking is often a necessity, being able to control an AI assistant hands-free can be a lifesaver. Gemini offers voice command functionality, making it even easier to integrate it into your daily routine.

Voice-Activated Control

With Gemini's voice capabilities, you can interact with the assistant without needing to type or tap on your device. Simply activate Gemini by saying "Hey Gemini," and then make your request, whether it's setting a reminder, asking for a weather update, or searching for a recipe.

This feature is particularly helpful when you're busy or on the go. For example, if you're driving, you can use voice commands to ask Gemini to read incoming messages, set a reminder, or get directions to your next appointment. Gemini's ability to listen and respond allows you to keep your hands free and focus on the task at hand.

Voice Assistance for Household Tasks

You can also integrate Gemini's voice commands into your daily household chores. For example, you can use Gemini to set timers when cooking, play music while you clean, or even control smart home devices if they are compatible. This hands-free capability makes Gemini an indispensable part of your day.

Google Gemini is more than just a chatbot; it's a comprehensive tool designed to assist with virtually every aspect of your daily life. From personal task management to hands-free operation, Gemini's capabilities are built to simplify your routine, help you stay organized, and keep you on track. Whether you're tackling your to-do list, summarizing content, planning your travel, or managing your shopping, Gemini is there to offer assistance at every turn. With its smart organization, time-saving features, and voice command functionality, Gemini proves to be an indispensable part of your digital toolkit.

Chapter 4

Supercharging Productivity with Gemini

In a world where efficiency dictates success, Gemini emerges not just as a supportive tool but as a game-changing digital ally. With the rise of remote work, content overload, and ever-increasing demands on time and focus, productivity isn't merely about getting things done—it's about getting the right things done faster and smarter. Google Gemini is designed precisely for this purpose. By blending artificial intelligence with Google's vast ecosystem, it brings automation, intelligent suggestions, real-time collaboration, and personal assistance into one seamless experience.

Automating Routine Tasks and Workflows

The most time-consuming tasks are often the ones we do repeatedly. These mundane processes—replying to common emails, entering data, formatting documents, scheduling updates—can eat up hours of your week without adding real value to your goals. Google Gemini steps in as a smart solution, identifying these patterns and offering automation that makes a real impact.

Gemini's automation capabilities are driven by contextual understanding. It doesn't just follow rigid rules like traditional automation tools; it understands intent. For example, if you consistently write a weekly summary for your team, Gemini can be trained through example prompts to automatically draft this summary based on your recent activity, shared documents, and emails.

You can also create workflow shortcuts by combining Gemini with other Google apps. Imagine a workflow where Gemini pulls your top 5 unread emails from Gmail, extracts key information, and generates action points in Google Tasks. Or a situation where it monitors a shared Drive folder and sends out automatic updates when a new document is added, complete with a brief summary for the team. These aren't far-fetched concepts—

they are realities with Gemini's AI automation layer.

Beyond individual use, Gemini can streamline team operations by setting up smart triggers. For example, when a new lead form is filled via Google Forms, Gemini can summarize the response, draft a follow-up email, schedule a call in Google Calendar, and notify the team in Google Chat—all within moments.

Scheduling Meetings, Generating Summaries, and Writing Drafts

Gemini's productivity toolkit shines when it comes to organizing your time and communication. Its scheduling prowess can significantly reduce the friction of aligning calendars and coordinating meetings. When you need to set a meeting with a colleague or multiple stakeholders, Gemini can scan available time slots across participants, suggest optimal times, and even draft the invitation with an agenda—all through a single command.

For instance, a prompt like, *"Schedule a 30-minute strategy call with Alice, John, and Ravi next week to discuss product roadmap updates"* will trigger Gemini to check everyone's calendars, find suitable time windows, and create a polished event description based on your context.

Gemini also excels at summarizing long content. Whether it's a dense email thread, a detailed article, or a lengthy meeting transcript, Gemini can generate bullet-point summaries or executive briefings in seconds. This is especially useful for managers who receive high volumes of information or for professionals who need to stay updated without investing hours into reading.

Its content generation abilities go even deeper. You can instruct Gemini to write everything from email responses and meeting minutes to blog post outlines and business reports. When writing drafts, Gemini isn't limited to generic text—it learns your tone, understands your objectives, and can mirror your brand voice with surprising precision. For example, it can craft a product announcement in a formal corporate tone or write a customer apology email that feels empathetic and human.

Real-Time Assistance in Google Docs and Sheets

Where Gemini truly redefines productivity is in its real-time integration with Google Workspace apps—particularly Docs and Sheets. Imagine having a digital collaborator who helps you brainstorm, structure, write, edit, and refine your content as you work. That's exactly what Gemini brings to Google Docs.

While typing a document, Gemini can suggest improvements to clarity, grammar, or tone—beyond what basic grammar checkers do. It can recommend alternative phrases for better impact, restructure sentences for logical flow, and even rewrite sections based on user feedback. For creators, marketers, and analysts, this is a huge time-saver.

For example, if you're drafting a project proposal, Gemini can help you:

- Generate an executive summary

- Suggest strong openers or closings

- Create a persuasive problem/solution framework

- Offer alternate headlines and bullet points

In Google Sheets, Gemini helps with everything from formula creation to data interpretation. If you're working on a sales tracker, Gemini can assist by analyzing trends, forecasting future metrics, or building pivot tables without complex commands. Simply type, *"Show a monthly breakdown of sales and highlight the top 3 performing regions,"* and Gemini takes over the heavy lifting.

The most powerful aspect is that Gemini understands the context within your documents. It doesn't just react to commands—it anticipates needs. If you mention a meeting in your document, Gemini might suggest adding it to your Calendar. If you refer to a file, it might offer a Drive link. This level of context-aware assistance streamlines multitasking and makes collaboration much more fluid.

Project Management Support and Smart Organization

Every successful project demands clear structure, timely updates, and strong communication. Gemini enhances all three by acting as a behind-the-scenes coordinator. Its ability to analyze, organize, and update across platforms makes it an ideal assistant for managing both solo and collaborative projects.

Start with planning. When outlining a new project, you can ask Gemini to help you define goals, milestones, and deadlines. It can create detailed Gantt chart outlines, suggest task dependencies, and even write up project scopes in a formal style. If you're using Google Sheets or Docs, these templates can be formatted instantly with customizable fields.

Next is task assignment. You can have Gemini help delegate responsibilities by analyzing your project plan and team members' roles. A simple prompt like, *"Assign tasks for our Q3 marketing launch based on team specialties,"* allows Gemini to draft a fair distribution of work, including timelines and accountability points.

During the execution phase, Gemini tracks progress by integrating with Google Tasks and Calendar. It can send reminders, generate progress reports, and summarize recent activity. Gemini also helps maintain clarity by creating update summaries for your team, pulling data from shared documents, and presenting it in digestible formats.

In fast-paced environments, keeping track of priorities is challenging. Gemini acts like a mental assistant—tagging urgent tasks, flagging overdue items, and even reordering to-dos based on your input or upcoming deadlines. This makes it easier to stay focused on what truly matters while avoiding last-minute scrambles.

Using Gemini as Your Personal Assistant

Gemini is more than a productivity tool—it's a personal AI companion that learns your work style, preferences, and routines. As a personal assistant, it can orchestrate your day, streamline your communication, and make intelligent recommendations tailored to your workflow.

Start your morning with a productivity dashboard. You can set Gemini to greet you each day with a summary of upcoming meetings, key deadlines, important emails, and even weather or traffic conditions. A command like, *"What do I need to focus on today?"* activates Gemini's full potential, pulling data from Calendar, Gmail, Tasks, and Drive to deliver a neatly organized agenda.

Throughout the day, Gemini helps minimize distractions by offering focus modes. For example, if you're in a deep work session, Gemini can pause non-critical notifications and log messages for later summarization. If you're stuck in decision fatigue, Gemini can present clear pros and cons, summaries of key info, or even quick polls for your team to vote on.

You can also train Gemini with specific preferences. Want emails drafted in a friendly but professional tone? Gemini will learn and replicate that tone across your communication. Prefer short meetings? Gemini can add time limits to your calendar events and include smart agendas to keep discussions on track.

As your personal assistant, Gemini even supports emotional and mental clarity. It can recommend productivity techniques like the Pomodoro method, remind you to take breaks, or help restructure an overwhelming day into manageable chunks. The AI isn't just assisting—it's learning, adapting, and evolving alongside you.

Google Gemini is not just about doing more; it's about doing better—with less effort. Its ability to automate tasks, manage schedules, assist in writing, and streamline collaboration transforms how professionals approach productivity. By becoming a true AI-powered assistant, Gemini doesn't just help you keep up—it helps you stay ahead.

Whether you're a solo entrepreneur juggling multiple hats or a corporate team player managing complex projects, Gemini fits your workflow and elevates your outcomes. It takes care of the small things so you can focus on big-picture thinking. In an era where time is the most valuable currency, Gemini becomes the productivity investment that keeps paying dividends.

Chapter 5

Creating Content with Gemini

In today's digital landscape, content is king—and creativity is the crown that sets it apart. From blog posts and social media updates to newsletters, video scripts, and polished ad copy, the pressure to consistently produce fresh, engaging material has never been higher. Fortunately, Google Gemini offers creators, marketers, and entrepreneurs a cutting-edge AI-powered assistant that helps transform vague ideas into polished, publishable content within minutes. It's not just about writing faster—it's about writing smarter, designing sharper, and delivering better.

Whether you're a content creator running a blog, a business owner managing email campaigns, or a digital marketer creating ad copy and visuals, Gemini becomes your always-on creative partner.

Writing Blog Posts, Social Captions, Emails, and Newsletters

Gemini's most immediate value for content creators lies in its ability to generate high-quality written content tailored for different formats and platforms. With a few simple prompts, Gemini can produce complete blog articles, engaging social media captions, effective email campaigns, and polished newsletters that align with your voice and audience.

Blog Posts

Creating blog posts typically involves multiple stages: topic selection, keyword alignment, structuring, drafting, and editing. Gemini simplifies each stage by guiding you from idea to execution. You can start with a simple prompt like, *"Write a 1,500-word blog post on the benefits of remote work for startups."* Gemini will generate a structured article with headings, subheadings, and smooth transitions.

Want something more specific? You can input detailed instructions such as tone (professional, casual, or humorous), target audience (tech founders, HR professionals), and preferred style (listicle, how-to guide, opinion piece). Gemini adapts its output accordingly and can even insert relevant keywords or internal links if you specify SEO requirements.

Social Media Captions

Gemini excels at short-form content too. For platforms like Instagram, Twitter, LinkedIn, or Facebook, you can instruct Gemini to generate platform-specific captions, complete with hashtags and call-to-actions (CTAs). For example, you might type, *"Create 5 Instagram captions for a bakery launching a new sourdough bread."* In return, Gemini might produce:

- "Say hello to our new love: Golden-crusted sourdough magic. Freshly baked, daily."

- "Crispy on the outside, soft on the inside. Meet our newest sourdough obsession. #FreshBread #SourdoughLove"

This fast generation capability is especially useful for scheduling weekly content calendars in advance or creating content for campaigns.

Emails and Newsletters

Gemini is highly effective in drafting promotional emails, customer service templates, onboarding sequences, and full-fledged newsletters. You can prompt it to create messages based on past campaigns or desired tone. A command like, *"Write a friendly newsletter introducing our summer product collection to loyal customers,"* will generate a structured piece complete with subject lines, greetings, product highlights, and a soft closing.

Better still, Gemini can integrate customer data from Google Sheets or Gmail to personalize emails with names, past purchases, or behavioral triggers. This is especially useful for marketers working with segmented audiences.

Brainstorming Ideas and Outlines

Sometimes the hardest part of content creation is figuring out where to begin. Gemini functions as a reliable brainstorming partner, helping you come up with new angles, themes, and structures. Whether you're stuck on what to write or how to say it, Gemini can unlock creative thinking by offering multiple directions to explore.

Idea Generation

Let's say you run a personal finance blog and need fresh topic ideas. You can prompt Gemini with, *"Give me 10 blog post ideas for a personal finance site targeting millennials."* You might get responses like:

- "How to Save for a House Without Giving Up Your Lifestyle"

- "Crypto or Stocks? The Millennial's Guide to Smart Investing"

- "Budgeting Apps That Actually Work in 2025"

These aren't just generic titles—they're refined based on trends, audience behavior, and tone preference if specified.

Gemini can also propose ideas based on seasonal themes, current events, or brand campaigns. Want to plan for Valentine's Day? Just ask: *"Suggest Valentine's Day campaign ideas for a skincare brand."*

Outlining Structures

Once you have a topic, Gemini can help map out a logical structure before writing. A prompt like, *"Create an outline for a blog post on sustainable fashion,"* will generate an organized framework:

1. Introduction to sustainable fashion

2. Why sustainability matters in clothing

3. Key materials and certifications to look for

4. Top 5 sustainable fashion brands in 2025

5. Tips for building an eco-friendly wardrobe

With this clear structure, writing becomes faster and more focused. You can even prompt Gemini to expand on each point one at a time, ensuring depth without drifting off-topic.

Enhancing Grammar, Tone, and Style

A key feature that sets Gemini apart from basic grammar tools is its ability to adapt content style and tone dynamically. Whether you're polishing a draft or transforming casual language into professional prose, Gemini becomes your intelligent editor.

Grammar and Sentence Structure

Gemini doesn't just fix typos. It rewrites sentences for clarity, conciseness, and fluency. You can paste a rough paragraph and ask Gemini to "make this more formal," "simplify for a younger audience," or "rephrase to sound confident." For example:

Original:

"We think our product might help improve your workflow, hopefully."

Refined by Gemini:

"Our product is designed to enhance your workflow with confidence."

This nuance makes Gemini ideal for professionals who need to maintain consistent tone across business communication, reports, or thought leadership articles.

Tone Adjustments

Whether you need a warm, inviting tone for a community newsletter or a direct, assertive tone for a policy update, Gemini tailors your message accordingly. A quick request like, *"Rewrite this paragraph in a friendly tone,"* can make technical content more approachable.

It also detects inconsistencies in tone within longer documents and suggests adjustments. For teams writing collaboratively, this ensures a unified voice across sections.

Style Enhancements

Gemini can emulate writing styles from famous personalities, industry voices, or even brand guides. Ask it to "write like Apple's marketing," or "sound like a TED Talk speaker," and it will modify vocabulary, pacing, and rhetorical devices to match.

It also handles multilingual content creation with ease. You can write in English and ask Gemini to translate your content into Spanish, French, or Hindi with context-specific adjustments to tone and slang.

Generating Creative Stories, Scripts, and Ad Copy

Beyond business and blogging, Gemini shines in creative tasks that require imagination and structure. Writers, content strategists, and advertisers can all use Gemini to rapidly ideate and produce compelling narratives, dialogue, or persuasive marketing content.

Stories and Narratives

Whether you're drafting a children's book, an emotional short story, or an interactive fiction experience, Gemini can help you write with emotion, creativity, and depth. Provide a prompt like, *"Write a short story about a child discovering a hidden world in their backyard,"* and Gemini will produce a well-structured narrative complete with character development, setting, conflict, and resolution.

You can even refine or continue the story with follow-up prompts: *"Make the tone more mysterious,"* or *"Add a twist ending."*

Scripts and Dialogue

For video content creators, YouTubers, and podcast hosts, Gemini offers scriptwriting capabilities. Give it a framework—such as an explainer video, comedy skit, or educational series—and it generates clean, engaging dialogue with proper timing cues. You can specify target length, mood, and pacing for more refined results.

A YouTube creator might prompt: *"Create a 5-minute video script introducing a new fitness app for beginners."*

Gemini will respond with:

- A hook to grab viewers' attention

- Logical flow between segments

- CTAs encouraging app downloads

- Optional B-roll suggestions if requested

Ad Copywriting

Marketers can harness Gemini's talent for producing ad headlines, email subject lines, PPC ad text, and persuasive CTAs. You can ask for multiple variations and test different tones—aggressive, emotional, benefit-driven, or humorous.

For instance: *"Create 5 Facebook ad headlines for a new vegan protein bar."*

Possible results:

- "Fuel Your Day, the Plant-Based Way"

- "Snack Clean. Feel Strong."

- "100% Vegan. 0% Boring."

Gemini can also help craft landing page copy, product descriptions, and A/B test variants to maximize conversion rates.

Designing with Gemini (Paired with Tools Like Canva or Google Slides)

Gemini doesn't design visuals directly like Photoshop or Canva, but it integrates with them by providing structured, well-written content, ideas, and layout guidance. It's the perfect co-creator when paired with design platforms.

Slide Content for Presentations

When creating slides in Google Slides, Gemini can generate outlines, bullet points, and even speaker notes. You can prompt:
"Create a 10-slide presentation on AI trends in healthcare with speaking points."

Gemini will:

- Provide slide titles and structured content per slide

- Suggest relevant stats and visuals

- Add speaker notes for each slide

This drastically speeds up the presentation design process and ensures clarity and professionalism.

Canva and Visual Content Guidance

For Canva users, Gemini can write the content you paste into templates—headlines, taglines, captions, banners, and descriptions. You can prompt: *"Create Instagram carousel text for a beauty brand sharing skincare tips."*

Gemini returns:

- Slide 1: "The Secret to Glowing Skin Starts Here..."

- Slide 2: "Tip #1: Hydration Over Everything"

- Slide 3: "Tip #2: Sunscreen Is Non-Negotiable"

You simply copy this into Canva and apply your design. Gemini can also recommend color palettes, font styles, and layout ideas if prompted, helping designers without formal training create polished content.

Gemini is revolutionizing the way creators approach content—from the first spark of an idea to the final polished product. Its ability to generate, edit, enhance, and organize across multiple formats makes it indispensable for professionals who need to produce high-quality output consistently and efficiently.

By streamlining everything from blog writing to ad scripting, email marketing to slide creation, Gemini becomes a co-writer, co-strategist, and creative muse. When paired with design tools, it transforms static visuals into powerful storytelling. For anyone working in content—whether full-time or as a side hustle—Gemini isn't just useful. It's essential.

Chapter 6

Prompting Power – How to Ask Gemini the Right Way

Understanding Prompt Structure and Clarity

The foundation of effective interaction with Gemini or any AI assistant lies in crafting prompts that are clear, structured, and purposeful. A prompt is essentially your instruction or question to the AI, and the quality of your result is directly tied to the quality of that input. When prompts are vague or ambiguous, the AI may generate generic or irrelevant responses. On the other hand, well-structured prompts that offer clarity, purpose, and context yield more accurate, coherent, and useful results.

A well-structured prompt includes a few key elements:

1. **Objective**: State clearly what you want Gemini to do. For example, "Summarize the following text" or "Write a professional email."
2. **Context**: Offer background or specific data Gemini needs to understand your request.
3. **Tone and Style**: Indicate the desired tone (formal, friendly, persuasive) and format (bullet points, paragraph, list).

4. **Constraints or Preferences**: If applicable, provide word limits, required elements, or what to avoid.

For example, instead of asking, "Write an email," ask: "Write a formal email to a potential client introducing our new digital marketing service. Keep it under 150 words and use a persuasive tone."

Examples of Effective vs. Poor Prompts

The difference between a successful prompt and a disappointing one often comes down to specificity. Let's examine a few scenarios to show the impact of precision and structure:

Example 1: Writing a Blog Introduction

- **Poor Prompt**: "Write an intro."

- **Effective Prompt**: "Write a 100-word introduction for a blog post titled '5 Ways Remote Work Boosts Productivity'. Use a friendly and informative tone to appeal to a young professional audience."

Example 2: Summarizing a Report

- **Poor Prompt**: "Summarize this."
- **Effective Prompt**: "Summarize the following 500-word market research report into 3 key insights suitable for a team meeting presentation."

Example 3: Creating Ad Copy

- **Poor Prompt**: "Make an ad."
- **Effective Prompt**: "Write a short, engaging Facebook ad copy for our new eco-friendly water bottle. Focus

on its sustainability benefits and target eco-conscious millennials. Keep it under 50 words."

The effective prompts guide Gemini more accurately and eliminate guesswork, allowing the AI to align its output with your intent.

Using Context to Guide Better AI Responses

Context is the bridge between your request and Gemini's understanding. The more relevant information you provide, the more Gemini can tailor its responses. When you include contextual clues, such as your audience, goals, background material, or existing content, Gemini is able to mimic the necessary style, structure, and depth.

Why Context Matters:

- Prevents generic or off-topic responses.
- Helps Gemini maintain consistency in tone and content.
- Enables more accurate interpretations of your goals.

Adding Context in Practice:

- **For email drafting**: Include who the recipient is, the reason for emailing, and any previous correspondence.
- **For article writing**: Provide your target audience, desired format, key points, and references.
- **For scripting**: Mention platform (YouTube, TikTok, etc.), tone (humorous, dramatic), and length.

Example: "I'm writing a LinkedIn post to share my excitement about joining a new company. The company is called BrightTech, and I joined as a Senior Data Analyst. I want the tone to be enthusiastic but professional, and I want to thank my previous employer. Please write the post."

Prompt Templates for Productivity, Content, Research, and Learning

To speed up your workflow and maintain consistency, use prompt templates. These are fill-in-the-blank structures that can be adapted to multiple tasks across areas like productivity, content creation, research, and learning.

Productivity Templates:

1. "Create a [checklist/plan/schedule] to help me [goal/task] within [timeframe]."
2. "Summarize my meeting notes below into key action items. [Insert text]"
3. "Generate a weekly agenda for a [type of team] focused on [project name]."

Content Creation Templates:

1. "Write a [type of content] on [topic] for [audience]. Include [keywords/style/CTA]."
2. "Create 5 social media captions for [platform] about [product or topic] using a [funny/informative/promotional] tone."

3. "Generate a content calendar for the next month with blog titles for a [niche] site."

Research Templates:

1. "Provide a summary of the latest trends in [industry/topic] with 3 cited sources."
2. "Compare [concept A] vs [concept B] in a table format highlighting pros and cons."
3. "List the top 10 books/articles on [subject] with brief descriptions."

Learning Templates:

1. "Explain [concept] in simple terms suitable for a [age group/education level]."

2. "Create a quiz with 5 questions to test knowledge on [topic]. Include answers."

3. "Build a study plan to learn [subject] over [timeframe] with daily topics."

Templates like these help you build consistent prompts that are immediately actionable and tailored to your needs, allowing you to use Gemini more effectively and reduce repetitive work.

Refining and Iterating Your Prompts for Best Results

The first prompt you use with Gemini may not always deliver exactly what you expect. That's why refining and iterating prompts is a critical part of getting the most out of your interaction. Iteration allows you to experiment with different wording, tones, or instructions to improve the results.

Step-by-Step Prompt Refinement:

1. **Review Output**: After the initial response, assess what worked and what didn't.

2. **Adjust Scope**: Narrow or broaden your request based on output length or depth.

3. **Tweak Tone or Style**: If tone feels off, revise with clearer style instructions.

4. **Include Missing Details**: If Gemini skipped points, specify those in your next prompt.

5. **Ask Follow-up Questions**: Use the initial result as a base for deeper exploration.

Example of Iteration:

- **Initial Prompt**: "Write a blog post on the benefits of meditation."
- **Result**: Too generic.
- **Refined Prompt**: "Write a 500-word blog post about the mental health benefits of daily meditation for working professionals, citing scientific studies, and using a calm and reassuring tone."
- **Further Refinement**: "Include a personal anecdote-style introduction and a bullet list of top benefits."

With each refinement, your prompt becomes more targeted and the output more relevant and valuable.

Prompt Iteration Tip: Think of Gemini like a collaborator. Just as you would provide feedback to a human colleague, give direction, clarify objectives, and work in steps to reach your ideal result.

Final Thoughts on Prompt Mastery

Mastering the art of prompting transforms Gemini from a basic assistant into a powerful productivity and creativity partner. Just like learning to code or write, prompt crafting is a skill that improves with practice. The better you are at expressing what you need—with structure, context, and clarity—the better Gemini becomes at delivering intelligent, precise, and innovative responses.

By applying these principles and using the templates provided, you'll develop the ability to:

- Save time across routine tasks
- Generate higher-quality content and ideas
- Enhance research and learning
- Communicate with AI in a way that feels intuitive and effective

Your relationship with AI is shaped by the questions you ask. So ask boldly, refine thoughtfully, and watch Gemini exceed your expectations.

Chapter 7

Gemini for Students, Teachers, and Lifelong Learners

The Intelligent Study Companion: Gemini's Role in Modern Education

Artificial intelligence is transforming the education landscape, and Google Gemini is leading this evolution by offering intelligent assistance to students, educators, and lifelong learners alike. From streamlining note-taking to guiding in-depth research, and from creating lesson plans to generating personalized explanations, Gemini serves as a comprehensive learning assistant across all academic levels.

In this chapter, we'll explore how Gemini can be integrated into daily academic routines, enhance classroom engagement, and support individual study goals, while also emphasizing the importance of ethical usage in educational environments.

Using Gemini for Studying, Summarizing, and Test Preparation

Smart Summaries for Smarter Studying

When facing a dense chapter, a long scientific paper, or an extended online article, Gemini can instantly generate concise, easy-to-understand summaries that break down complex content. Students can upload text or provide links, and Gemini will analyze the material to highlight key concepts, arguments, and conclusions. This becomes particularly helpful in subjects such as history, biology, or literature, where understanding core themes and structures is essential.

Flashcards, Definitions, and Study Aids

Gemini can convert notes into digital flashcards, simplifying the process of repetition and memorization. By turning bullet points into question-answer formats, students can actively test their understanding of a subject. Additionally, Gemini can define technical terms, provide etymologies, and even offer pronunciation assistance for language learners.

For example, inputting "Create flashcards for the main causes of World War I" will result in a neatly structured set of cards with trigger questions like "What was the role of the Alliance System in WWI?"

Personalized Test Preparation and Quizzes

Gemini can simulate exam-like conditions by generating custom quizzes based on a student's syllabus, textbook, or past papers. For subjects like math, Gemini can generate problems of varying difficulty and provide step-by-step solutions. In language subjects, it can quiz vocabulary, grammar rules, and reading comprehension. This adaptability makes it a go-to prep tool for anything from pop quizzes to standardized tests like the SAT, IELTS, or GRE.

Research Support with Citations and Explanations

Finding Credible Sources and Academic Materials

Gemini helps students save time by suggesting trustworthy sources when conducting academic research. By simply stating a topic like "climate change impact on agriculture in Africa," Gemini can suggest recent peer-reviewed articles, official reports, and recognized journal entries. It also provides guidance on how to cite them properly in APA, MLA, or Chicago styles.

Simplifying Complex Topics with Contextual Explanations

Academic texts can be intimidating, especially when they involve statistical data, scientific jargon, or philosophical arguments. Gemini excels at breaking down these complexities into digestible explanations without diluting accuracy. For instance, a student studying quantum mechanics could ask, "Explain Schrödinger's equation in simple terms," and Gemini would offer a coherent analogy or simplified breakdown that maintains the core concept.

Supporting Multilingual Research

Students who are non-native English speakers or who conduct research across languages can benefit from Gemini's multilingual abilities. It can translate scholarly content, explain idiomatic expressions, and help with paraphrasing content for academic integrity.

Lesson Plan and Worksheet Creation for Educators

Designing Lesson Plans from Scratch

Teachers no longer need to start every lesson plan from a blank page. Gemini can assist in creating tailored lesson plans based on curriculum requirements, class grade level, and learning objectives. A teacher can simply prompt, "Create a 45-minute lesson plan on the water cycle for Grade 5," and Gemini will outline a structured session including an introduction, interactive activities, key discussion points, and assessment methods.

Customizing Worksheets and Homework

Gemini enables educators to generate custom worksheets, assignments, and take-home exercises in seconds. Whether it's a grammar worksheet for ESL students or a math sheet on fractions, Gemini can format and diversify the content to fit the student's level of understanding.

The AI can also include answer keys and grading rubrics, saving teachers significant time on administrative tasks. This allows more energy to be spent on actual teaching and student engagement.

Creating Interactive Digital Content

For educators who use digital platforms, Gemini can generate slideshows, visual aids, and even quiz forms compatible with Google Forms or Docs. Teachers can request, "Create a 10-question multiple-choice quiz on renewable energy with answers," and Gemini will instantly produce a ready-to-use assessment tool.

Creative Classroom Applications of Gemini

Storytelling and Writing Support

Gemini brings creativity into the classroom by helping students brainstorm story ideas, develop characters, or even co-write short stories and poems. It can suggest plot twists, themes, and stylistic improvements to help students refine their writing.

Creative writing prompts like "Write a story about a robot in the year 3050 learning to feel emotions" can generate imaginative outputs that serve as either inspiration or a writing companion to push students' narrative skills.

Visual Learning with Multimodal Capabilities

By uploading images—such as diagrams, maps, or lab results—students can ask Gemini to analyze, describe, or interpret the visual data. For example, uploading a photo of a geometric shape can result in Gemini identifying it, explaining its properties, and suggesting problems related to the shape.

Collaborative Projects and Peer Reviews

Gemini supports group work by helping students divide tasks, schedule check-ins, and keep track of project deadlines. It can also assist in peer review exercises by providing suggestions for improving tone, grammar, structure, and clarity without rewriting the student's voice.

Avoiding Misuse: Understanding Ethics and Academic Integrity

AI as a Learning Tool, Not a Shortcut

While Gemini offers significant advantages, it is essential for students to understand that AI is a supportive tool—not a replacement for learning. Relying solely on AI to complete assignments, write essays, or generate test answers undermines the purpose of education. Gemini should be used to clarify doubts, enhance understanding, and assist creativity, not to bypass effort or academic responsibility.

Proper Attribution and Plagiarism Awareness

Gemini is capable of paraphrasing and summarizing content, but students must still credit original sources when required. Academic institutions often have strict plagiarism policies, and AI-generated content is not exempt. Gemini helps reduce the risk of accidental plagiarism by guiding proper citation, but students should always double-check for originality and authenticity.

Educators and AI Monitoring

Teachers also have a role in modeling ethical AI use. By showing students how to use Gemini for legitimate purposes—such as brainstorming, revising, or organizing—they can foster digital literacy and critical thinking. Many schools may also implement

AI-use policies, and Gemini can assist educators in drafting these guidelines.

Empowering Lifelong Learners with AI

Skill Development for Adults and Professionals

Gemini is not just for K-12 or college students. Adult learners seeking to master new skills—whether coding, photography, or business management—can use Gemini as a guide. It can recommend structured learning paths, summarize tutorials, and explain technical concepts in relatable ways. For instance, a user can prompt, "Teach me Python for data analysis," and receive a learning sequence with hands-on examples and recommended resources.

Personalized Learning Journeys

Unlike traditional courses, Gemini adapts to the learner's pace and preferences. It allows users to ask follow-up questions, go deeper into niche topics, or shift directions entirely. Lifelong learners can use it as a personalized tutor that's available 24/7, offering coaching that evolves with their curiosity and goals.

Learning in Micro-Moments

With Gemini on mobile devices, learners can absorb knowledge during commutes, breaks, or while doing chores—turning idle moments into opportunities for growth. Whether it's a language learner practicing phrases, or a professional catching up on industry news, Gemini brings learning into everyday life.

A New Era of Smart Learning

Google Gemini redefines what it means to study, teach, and learn in a connected, AI-powered world. It makes information more accessible, learning more personalized, and teaching more creative. Whether you're a high school student prepping for exams, a college professor designing a syllabus, or a retiree diving into a new subject, Gemini empowers you with tools to achieve more—efficiently, ethically, and enjoyably.

The real magic of Gemini in education lies not just in automation but in amplification. It amplifies your curiosity, creativity, and capacity to understand the world around you. And as you turn each page in your learning journey, Gemini remains a steady, intelligent companion—always ready to help you learn smarter.

Chapter 8

Gemini in the Workplace and Business

Transforming Work Culture with Google Gemini

The digital workplace is evolving rapidly, and artificial intelligence is becoming central to how businesses function, communicate, and grow. Google Gemini, integrated across Google Workspace, is designed to be more than a digital assistant—it is a powerful productivity and business enhancement tool that streamlines processes, improves decision-making, and fuels creativity.

From startups to large corporations, Gemini can significantly reduce the time spent on routine tasks while amplifying strategic planning, customer engagement, and cross-functional collaboration.

Enhancing Team Collaboration Through Smart AI

Real-Time Document Collaboration and Smart Suggestions

Collaboration is at the heart of modern work, and Gemini enhances it with context-aware intelligence. Integrated directly into Google Docs, Sheets, Slides, and Gmail, Gemini actively assists team members working on shared projects.

As collaborators type into a shared Google Doc, Gemini can highlight inconsistencies, suggest rewording, summarize discussions, and recommend citations or relevant links. For example, in a live brainstorming document, team members can use prompts like, "Summarize the three ideas above," and Gemini will instantly produce a cohesive paragraph that aligns with the team's tone and direction.

This is especially beneficial in asynchronous work environments where team members may be in different time zones. Gemini ensures continuity by acting as a silent contributor who never misses a detail.

Smart Email Drafts and Thread Summarization in Gmail

Business communication via email often consumes hours of valuable time. Gemini shortens this with intelligent draft creation and email thread summarization. If a team member has been out of office and returns to a long email chain, they can prompt Gemini with, "Summarize this conversation and highlight the final decision," and receive a clear, concise overview.

Moreover, Gemini can draft professional emails based on prompts like, "Write a follow-up email after a sales demo," ensuring tone, structure, and purpose are aligned with the recipient.

Meeting Summaries and Action Items

During meetings on Google Meet, Gemini can act as a silent observer that listens and takes notes in real time. Post-meeting, it can generate structured summaries, capture key decisions, and automatically assign action items based on who said what.

Teams no longer need a designated note-taker, and nobody misses out if they're late or absent. Gemini can even sync with Google Tasks or Calendar to ensure follow-ups are scheduled appropriately.

Creating Business Plans, Reports, and Meeting Notes

From Vision to Execution: Writing Business Plans with Gemini

Whether you're a startup founder or a project manager, drafting a business plan is a critical yet time-consuming task. Gemini can generate detailed plans based on your input regarding goals, target markets, competition, and operational strategy.

Prompt: "Create a business plan for a home-based catering service targeting corporate events in Lagos."

Gemini will output a structured document including an executive summary, market analysis, marketing strategy, financial projections, and growth roadmap. You can then customize, fine-tune, and expand each section according to investor or partner requirements.

Professional Report Writing Made Effortless

Writing reports—be it weekly updates, project progress, or financial analyses—often requires both factual accuracy and professional polish. Gemini can assist by turning bullet points, spreadsheets, or even meeting notes into formal reports.

For instance, after inputting performance data into Google Sheets, you can prompt Gemini with, "Create a quarterly performance summary based on this sheet," and it will produce a structured report, including visualizations, KPIs, and interpretations.

Meeting Agendas and Notes

Creating meeting agendas is crucial to ensure focused discussions. Gemini can generate them from scratch based on past meeting topics, emails, or ongoing projects. After the meeting, it can also document notes, assign responsibilities, and share them with relevant stakeholders—automating an essential yet repetitive workflow.

Generating Customer Service Replies and Product Descriptions

Elevating Customer Support with Gemini

Customer service agents often need to respond to repetitive queries quickly and consistently. Gemini can generate pre-written response templates for common questions, allowing agents to personalize them as needed.

For example, if a customer writes, "I didn't receive my order," an agent can prompt Gemini with, "Draft a polite response offering a refund or reshipment for a delayed order." Gemini ensures tone-appropriate and professional replies every time, reducing response time and increasing satisfaction.

It also helps maintain brand voice consistency across responses by using predefined tone settings—friendly, formal, empathetic, or solution-focused.

Automated FAQ Creation

Gemini can analyze a business's most common customer inquiries—sourced from email threads, chat logs, or help desk software—and generate a comprehensive FAQ document. This is extremely useful for scaling businesses that want to set up knowledge bases or self-service support portals.

Writing Compelling Product Descriptions

Product descriptions are vital for e-commerce businesses, and Gemini can generate compelling, SEO-friendly descriptions tailored to different platforms like Shopify, Amazon, or Etsy.

Prompt: "Write a product description for a handmade lavender soy candle, targeting eco-conscious buyers."

Gemini will provide descriptions that highlight features, benefits, sustainability, and emotional appeal, which can be adjusted for tone or length depending on platform requirements.

Small Business Use: Content Marketing, Social Media, and Scheduling

Content Marketing Made Scalable

Gemini can be a small business's secret weapon for content marketing. It generates blog posts, newsletters, email sequences, and lead magnets from simple prompts.

For instance, inputting "Write a blog post on 5 easy vegetarian recipes for busy professionals" will yield a structured post with an engaging title, subheadings, list format, and call-to-action. Business owners can further enhance it with Gemini's suggestions for keywords, hashtags, or internal linking.

Social Media Strategy and Execution

Managing a brand's presence on social media requires both strategy and consistency. Gemini helps by generating platform-specific captions, image ideas, hashtags, and posting calendars.

You can prompt Gemini with, "Generate a week's worth of Instagram posts for a fitness coach promoting a 30-day challenge," and receive daily posts with unique themes, captions, and call-to-actions.

It also helps repurpose content across platforms. A YouTube video summary can become a LinkedIn article, an Instagram carousel, and an email teaser—all with Gemini's help.

Scheduling and Time Management

Gemini can create a weekly content calendar, track promotional campaigns, and set reminders for publication deadlines by integrating with Google Calendar and Tasks.

Prompt: "Schedule three weekly posts for the month of June promoting summer skincare products," and Gemini will generate a campaign with suggested posting dates, themes, and formats. It also sends follow-up reminders and adjusts based on new launches or holidays.

Integrating Gemini into Workflows Using Workspace Tools

Deep Integration with Google Docs, Sheets, and Slides

Gemini is embedded within the fabric of Google Workspace, making it easier to work without switching apps. In Google Docs, Gemini suggests grammar fixes, rewrites unclear sentences, generates outlines, and offers real-time feedback.

In Google Sheets, it can analyze data, create pivot tables, generate graphs, and even interpret trends with simple prompts like, "Explain the drop in sales in Q2."

In Google Slides, Gemini can draft an entire presentation, including slide titles, bullet points, visual design suggestions, and speaker notes. You can start with, "Create a 10-slide presentation on market expansion strategies for Southeast Asia," and Gemini will return a draft that's ready to polish.

Using Gemini in Google Meet and Calendar

Gemini integrates with Calendar to automatically schedule meetings based on availability, send reminders, and suggest optimal time slots based on past scheduling behavior.

During Google Meet sessions, it can capture live captions, transcribe discussions, and send summaries to attendees. Prompting it with "What were the action items from today's sales sync?" after a meeting results in a well-organized list of follow-ups.

Automating Workflows with Gemini and Google Apps Script

For users with technical inclination, Gemini can be paired with Google Apps Script to automate repetitive workflows. For instance, it can write scripts to:

- Send weekly reports from Sheets to Gmail

- Archive old files in Drive

- Trigger auto-reminders for task deadlines

Even if users aren't coders, Gemini can generate the script code with a simple prompt like, "Create a script that sends an email when a row in Google Sheets is updated."

Future-Ready Business with AI-Powered Productivity

As businesses continue to adapt to hybrid work, remote teams, and digital-first operations, tools like Gemini are not optional—they are essential. They reduce inefficiencies, eliminate friction, and provide real-time support that enhances both individual and organizational performance.

Whether you're leading a sales team, running a one-person online store, or managing a corporate department, Gemini becomes a digital extension of your business strategy. It enables faster execution, deeper insights, and better customer connection.

Gemini as a Business Game-Changer

Gemini is not just another AI assistant. It's a versatile, deeply integrated business companion that transforms how work gets done. From internal collaboration and strategic documentation to external communications and brand presence, Gemini redefines efficiency in a modern business context.

By embedding Gemini into your daily business processes, you're not only saving time—you're unlocking the next level of operational excellence. And as AI continues to evolve, Gemini stands ready to evolve with you, ensuring your business stays ahead of the curve.

Chapter 9

Exploring Gemini Advanced (Gemini 1.5 Pro)

The Next Evolution of AI Assistance

As the world increasingly embraces artificial intelligence to streamline everyday tasks, Google continues to raise the bar with its most advanced AI offering: **Gemini Advanced**, powered by **Gemini 1.5 Pro**. This new tier represents a monumental leap from earlier models, integrating unparalleled reasoning abilities, extended memory capabilities, and the power to perform complex operations with remarkable context sensitivity. While the free version of Gemini handles many general productivity tasks, Gemini Advanced is designed for users who demand depth, precision, and intelligence across highly nuanced domains.

Whether you're a researcher, developer, data analyst, creative professional, or business strategist, Gemini Advanced opens a new frontier in AI productivity.

What Is Gemini Advanced and What Makes It Powerful?

Introducing Gemini 1.5 Pro: A Smarter, Longer-Memory AI

Gemini Advanced is built on Google's **Gemini 1.5 Pro model**, which dramatically enhances the capabilities of the standard Gemini version. It is designed to think more critically, analyze with more depth, and recall more context than ever before. In practical terms, this means it can retain and reason over larger documents, conduct deeper research analysis, and complete multi-step tasks with better accuracy and coherence.

One of the most defining features of Gemini Advanced is its **context window**, which allows it to process and understand up to **1 million tokens** in a single conversation. This dwarfs the capabilities of most AI models and enables Gemini Advanced to work with book-length texts, long legal documents, intricate coding tasks, and massive datasets without losing track of the narrative or logic.

Designed for Professionals and Power Users

While casual users benefit from Gemini's quick answers and content generation, Gemini Advanced is tailored for users with complex needs:

- **Academics and researchers** can feed entire PDFs and get structured critiques or summaries.

- **Programmers** can debug thousands of lines of code in one interaction.

- **Writers and content strategists** can maintain coherent plots across novel-length manuscripts.

- **Enterprise users** can manage in-depth workflows, analyze policies, or generate high-level business reports.

Gemini Advanced is not just more powerful—it's more **conversational**, **intent-aware**, and **solution-oriented**, capable of thinking through ambiguity, understanding user goals, and proposing intelligent next steps.

Key Upgrades: Longer Context, Deeper Understanding

The Power of Extended Context

The extended context window—up to **1 million tokens** (or roughly 750,000 words)—is a game-changer. For comparison, most standard AI models can only handle between 4,000 and 32,000 tokens at a time. With Gemini Advanced:

- You can upload **entire books, websites, or large datasets**, and ask questions about any section.

- You can provide **multi-layered prompts** that build on each other without having to restate prior inputs.

- You can develop **strategic plans, research papers, and software** with a level of coherence and memory continuity previously impossible.

This extended memory also makes it suitable for legal professionals reviewing case law, analysts exploring market reports, or educators working through multiple lesson units at once.

Reasoning Across Complex Topics

Gemini 1.5 Pro is designed to understand **interdependencies between facts**, **contextual intent**, and **subtle nuances** in text or code. It does not merely retrieve answers but reasons them out.

For instance, when asked to analyze the impact of rising interest rates on small business credit access, Gemini Advanced can:

- Incorporate data from economic reports

- Interpret regulatory language

- Compare current and historical trends

- Generate a plain-English summary

- Offer actionable insights and mitigation strategies

This deep understanding makes Gemini a critical thinking partner, not just a writing assistant.

Multimodal Awareness (Text, Code, Images)

Gemini Advanced is multimodal, meaning it can handle and cross-reference **text, images, diagrams, and code** within the same interaction. You could:

- Upload a chart and ask for interpretation trends

- Submit a diagram and ask for workflow automation suggestions

- Paste in raw code and receive optimized alternatives

The model can also **generate visual content ideas**, provide **design critiques**, or interpret **scientific graphs** embedded in documents, making it an all-in-one intelligence engine.

How to Access Gemini Advanced via Google One

The Google One AI Premium Plan

To unlock Gemini Advanced, users must subscribe to the **Google One AI Premium Plan**, introduced as a premium-tier service offering access to Gemini 1.5 Pro. The subscription includes:

- Full access to Gemini Advanced via the web and mobile apps

- Gemini features integrated into **Gmail, Docs, Sheets, Slides, and Meet**

- **2TB of Google Drive storage**

- Additional Google One benefits, such as advanced photo editing in Google Photos

As of 2025, the monthly subscription is competitively priced and offers significant value for professionals seeking a robust AI companion across personal and business workflows.

Activation Steps

1. **Sign in to your Google account** and go to the Google One website.

2. Choose the **AI Premium Plan** from the available subscriptions.

3. Complete your payment and confirm activation.

4. Access **Gemini Advanced** via the dedicated Gemini app or through Workspace integrations.

Once subscribed, your account is upgraded across all connected Google services, and you gain priority access to new AI features and future Gemini updates.

Real-World Tasks Gemini 1.5 Handles Better

Document Analysis and Summarization

Gemini Advanced can consume and analyze **full-length research papers**, **legal contracts**, or **business reports** in one go. It can:

- Summarize each section

- Extract key statistics and findings

- Compare it with another document

- Suggest editorial improvements

It's perfect for professionals who routinely work with large text-based content and need distilled, meaningful output quickly.

Coding and Debugging at Scale

Developers benefit immensely from Gemini Advanced's ability to:

- Interpret thousands of lines of code

- Spot errors, security risks, or inefficiencies

- Suggest refactoring and optimization strategies

- Write documentation based on code structure

It can also support **multi-language development environments**, making it a flexible assistant for full-stack programmers, DevOps engineers, and software testers.

Brainstorming and Creative Writing

Writers often face challenges maintaining consistency across long-form content. Gemini Advanced allows you to:

- Develop characters and arcs for an entire novel

- Maintain thematic cohesion across chapters

- Receive critiques or tone suggestions

- Generate outlines, scenes, and dialogues with memory of prior elements

It acts as a persistent writing partner that remembers the context you built weeks ago.

Data Interpretation and Strategy Planning

Whether you're analyzing market research, building a business expansion plan, or managing a large event, Gemini Advanced can process:

- Excel and Google Sheets files with thousands of entries

- Graphs, charts, and trend reports

- Survey or customer feedback results

You can request, "Summarize customer sentiment across this 50,000-row dataset," and Gemini will return trends, insights, and suggestions for next steps.

Limitations and Ethical Considerations of Advanced AI

Current Limitations

Despite its vast capabilities, Gemini Advanced still has limitations:

- **Latency**: Processing large inputs can sometimes result in longer response times.

- **Dependence on Prompts**: While smarter, Gemini still needs clear prompts for optimal results.

- **Factual Accuracy**: Like all LLMs, it may still produce plausible but incorrect or outdated information if not grounded in real-time data.

- **Lack of Real-World Awareness**: Gemini doesn't "know" current news unless fed through documents or queries via APIs.

Users should always **verify critical outputs**, especially for legal, medical, or financial decisions.

Ethical Use and Academic Integrity

As AI becomes more powerful, so does the need for responsible use. Some key areas of ethical concern include:

- **Plagiarism**: Users must avoid submitting AI-generated work as their own in academic or creative contexts.

- **Misinformation**: AI-generated content should be fact-checked to avoid spreading incorrect data.

- **Bias and Fairness**: Gemini Advanced, like other models, is trained on large internet datasets and may occasionally reflect biased or stereotypical views.

Google has built-in tools to report harmful outputs and improve transparency. Users are also encouraged to disclose AI assistance when appropriate and ensure that human oversight remains central to decision-making.

Unlocking the Full Potential of Gemini

Gemini Advanced marks a pivotal evolution in how AI can augment human intelligence. With the unmatched capabilities of Gemini 1.5 Pro, professionals in every domain—from software to education, business to creative arts—can now rely on AI not just to assist, but to **collaborate** intelligently and contextually.

Whether you're summarizing massive reports, analyzing codebases, writing books, or crafting strategy documents, Gemini Advanced adapts to your needs and evolves with your workflows. It's more than just a tool—it's a strategic partner for the AI-driven era.

As AI continues to shape the future of work, creativity, and innovation, those who understand and harness the full capabilities of Gemini Advanced will be better equipped to lead, adapt, and thrive in an increasingly intelligent world.

Chapter 10

Beyond Text – Multimodal Magic of Gemini

The Rise of Multimodal AI

In the rapidly evolving world of artificial intelligence, the leap from purely text-based models to multimodal capabilities marks a defining milestone. Google's Gemini, especially in its advanced versions, doesn't just understand words—it interprets images, listens to audio, and can analyze videos. This multimodal power propels Gemini into a new realm of usefulness, one that bridges communication gaps and enhances human creativity in ways never before imagined. No longer limited to chat-like interactions, Gemini becomes a multi-sensory AI capable of acting as an intelligent collaborator across text, visuals, and sound.

Gemini's Ability to Understand Images, Audio, and Video

Breaking the Modality Barrier

Gemini's multimodal capabilities allow it to interpret and respond to inputs from various formats. This includes:

- **Images**: Gemini can process visual information, identify objects, extract text, analyze design elements, and understand visual storytelling.

- **Audio**: It can interpret spoken language, identify speakers, understand tone and emotion, and even transcribe or summarize audio content.

- **Video**: Gemini understands video files by combining its ability to process sequential image frames and audio tracks. This allows it to summarize, interpret, or comment on video content with impressive accuracy.

This rich integration of sensory inputs equips Gemini to handle more human-like communication scenarios, mirroring the way people use multiple senses to interpret the world.

Model Architecture Supporting Multimodal Understanding

At its core, Gemini's ability to process multimodal data stems from its transformer-based architecture that has been trained on massive datasets containing not just text, but labeled images, audio, and video sequences. It uses a combination of convolutional neural networks (CNNs) for visual understanding and transformers for contextual interpretation, making it well-suited for:

- Visual recognition and captioning

- Scene detection and object classification

- Audio transcription and emotion detection

- Video event recognition and timeline summarization

This synergy between modalities allows Gemini to generate contextually appropriate and highly intelligent responses regardless of input type.

Uploading Files and Receiving Smart Analysis

File Input Options

Gemini supports a wide range of input formats, making it easy to interact using your preferred file type. Users can upload directly through:

- **Google Drive Integration**: Seamless access to stored images, audio recordings, and videos.

- **Direct Upload via Gemini Interface**: Drag-and-drop or file selection options within the Gemini chat or app.

- **Gmail and Docs**: Embedding visual/audio content within documents or emails for instant interpretation.

Types of Analysis Gemini Performs

1. Image Analysis

- **Object Detection**: Identifies objects, landmarks, faces, and text within images.

- **Scene Description**: Provides contextual descriptions of scenes or visual environments.

- **Design Critique**: Evaluates balance, color harmony, layout structure, and aesthetics.

- **Medical and Scientific Images**: Can interpret X-rays, charts, diagrams, and lab visuals (within limits).

2. Audio Analysis

- **Speech Recognition**: Transcribes audio into text, distinguishing between speakers and languages.

- **Tone and Sentiment**: Detects emotional cues and conversational dynamics.

- **Audio Summarization**: Condenses long recordings into digestible summaries.

- **Music Understanding**: Recognizes instruments, genre, and rhythm patterns (still in experimental stages).

3. Video Analysis

- **Scene Segmentation**: Breaks videos into key events or transitions.

- **Dialogue Extraction**: Pulls spoken parts into readable transcripts.

- **Narrative Understanding**: Offers summaries, character identification, or plot structure.

- **Instructional Videos**: Can extract steps from how-to videos for documentation.

User Interface and Feedback

Gemini's file analysis interface provides:

- **Thumbnail Previews** for uploaded media

- **Step-by-step analysis** as results are processed

- **Interactive Q&A** based on media content

Users can follow up with questions like "What are the key themes in this video?" or "Can you describe the color palette used in this graphic?" to refine or expand on the analysis.

Example Use Cases: Interpreting Images and Visual Project Help

Use Case 1: Educational Illustration Analysis

Teachers can upload textbook diagrams or infographics and ask Gemini to:

- Label parts of the diagram

- Explain concepts visually

- Translate visuals into text-based explanations for visually impaired students

Use Case 2: Real Estate Photo Reviews

Real estate agents upload property photos, and Gemini:

- Identifies key features (kitchen design, natural lighting)

- Suggests selling points based on layout and finish

- Flags potential issues (cracks, poor lighting, clutter)

Use Case 3: Product Photography Critique

E-commerce entrepreneurs upload product shots to receive:

- Suggestions on angles and lighting

- Recommendations for editing

- Text for product descriptions based on visual attributes

Use Case 4: UI/UX Design Feedback

Designers provide screenshots or prototypes, and Gemini:

- Assesses usability and layout clarity

- Suggests color or contrast improvements

- Highlights accessibility issues

Use Case 5: Video Tutorials Summarization

Content creators submit recorded screen tutorials, and Gemini:

- Extracts steps performed

- Generates a step-by-step guide

- Summarizes video into a blog post or instruction sheet

These use cases demonstrate Gemini's transformative role in bridging visual content and actionable insights, reducing the gap between creation and interpretation.

AI as a Visual and Creative Collaborator

Ideation Through Visual Prompts

Gemini can help users brainstorm ideas by interpreting mood boards, sketches, or reference images. For example:

- Fashion designers can upload fabric patterns and receive suggestions on garment combinations.

- Architects can input 3D models or layout sketches to brainstorm design improvements.

- Artists can present incomplete pieces and receive theme suggestions or style comparisons.

Visual Storyboarding and Illustration Support

Writers and directors can:

- Upload concept art or rough storyboards

- Ask Gemini to suggest visual transitions or narrative pacing

- Generate written scenes based on visual stimuli

Marketing and Branding Assistance

Businesses can refine their visual identity using Gemini:

- Evaluate logo designs

- Ensure visual consistency across social media content

- Suggest imagery to match brand tone

Accessibility Partner

Gemini aids in creating accessible content by:

- Generating alt-text for images automatically

- Describing complex visuals in plain language

- Translating audio descriptions for videos into captions or transcripts

Mixed Media Project Development

Gemini can integrate text, audio, and visual planning for:

- Multimedia presentations

- Interactive learning modules

- Cross-platform ad campaigns

A Multi-Sensory Future for AI

The future of artificial intelligence is not confined to words alone. Gemini's multimodal capabilities exemplify how next-generation AI will function as a truly perceptive partner—seeing, hearing, and interpreting the world as humans do. This positions Gemini not just as a tool, but as a **co-creator**, **collaborator**, and **interpreter** across various sensory dimensions.

As users explore and adopt these capabilities, they stand to gain a revolutionary edge in creativity, productivity, and communication. By harnessing the power of multimodal AI, we move one step closer to a reality where digital assistance mirrors the richness of human perception and thought.

Chapter 11

Comparing Gemini with Other AI Tools

The Expanding AI Landscape

Artificial Intelligence has evolved into a competitive ecosystem where innovation is constant and the boundaries of what's possible are being redrawn almost daily. Among the dominant players are **Google Gemini**, **OpenAI's ChatGPT**, **Anthropic's Claude**, and **Microsoft Copilot**. Each AI tool brings its own unique strengths, underlying architectures, and use-case specialties. While they may appear similar on the surface, a deeper comparison reveals key differences in their functionality, user experience, data handling, integration capabilities, and more. For users seeking the best tool for productivity, creativity, business, or learning, understanding how these AIs stack up against one another is essential.

Gemini vs ChatGPT: A Rivalry Rooted in Innovation

Origins and Design Philosophies

ChatGPT, developed by OpenAI, became the first AI tool to reach widespread public acclaim for its conversational tone and natural language fluency. Based on the GPT (Generative Pre-trained Transformer) architecture, ChatGPT excels in generating coherent, contextually rich responses to a wide range of prompts. It powers everything from casual conversations to complex business writing.

On the other hand, **Gemini**, Google's successor to Bard, is designed with a clear vision of integrating AI within the broader Google ecosystem. Backed by Gemini 1.0 and the more advanced Gemini 1.5 Pro, its focus goes beyond conversation — aiming at productivity, multimodal interaction, deep information recall, and contextual analysis.

Core Strengths Comparison

Feature	ChatGPT (GPT-4)	Google Gemini

Language Fluency	Exceptionally coherent and creative	Accurate, context-rich
Web Integration	Limited real-time browsing (paid)	Built-in Google Search access
Document Integration	Manual input only	Native integration with Gmail, Docs, Drive
Multimodal Capabilities	Images (Pro version), plugins	Natively supports image, video, audio input

Interface	App and Web	App, Web, Android, iOS integration
Memory/ Context Handling	Up to 128K tokens	Up to 1 million tokens (Gemini 1.5 Pro)
Personalization	Moderate	High, tied to your Google account
Real-Time Collaboration	Limited	Built for Workspace collaboration

Gemini edges out in ecosystem compatibility and real-time document interaction, while ChatGPT maintains an edge in conversational tone and creativity.

Gemini vs Claude: Ethically Driven Intelligence

Claude, created by Anthropic, is built on the idea of "constitutional AI" — a model that prioritizes safety, transparency, and ethical reasoning. It aims to make AI behavior more predictable and safe by training the model with a set of guiding principles rather than relying solely on reinforcement learning.

Areas Where Claude Shines

Claude stands out in situations where ethical nuance, safe content moderation, and sensitive dialogue are required. It's well-suited for educational platforms, mental health support, and environments where responsible AI use is paramount. Its responses often include disclaimers, citations, or clarification if a user's query veers into ethically ambiguous territory.

Gemini in Comparison

While Gemini also prioritizes ethical AI use — with safety mechanisms baked into its responses — it focuses more on **productivity-enhancing utility** than deep ethical alignment. Its strength lies in real-world usage: summarizing Google Docs, interpreting YouTube videos, enhancing email drafts, and facilitating meetings.

If your priority is **work output, personal organization, and integrated productivity**, Gemini leads. But if you're designing for environments where **ethical reasoning and caution** are critical, Claude may be a better fit.

Gemini vs Microsoft Copilot: The Corporate Powerhouse

Microsoft Copilot, powered by OpenAI's GPT technology, is integrated deeply into Microsoft 365. It acts as a writing, summarizing, and analysis assistant within tools like Word, Excel, Outlook, and Teams. Unlike ChatGPT, Copilot's edge is **native embedding in workplace applications**.

Enterprise Integration

Copilot's deep hooks into Excel and PowerPoint allow it to do things like:

- Automatically generate presentations from bullet points.

- Suggest formulas in Excel.

- Summarize Teams meeting notes in Outlook.

- Draft documents based on reference materials.

How Gemini Competes

Gemini's **strength is agility** — it integrates across Gmail, Google Docs, Calendar, Sheets, Drive, and even YouTube. But it also goes further, offering multimodal abilities, image and video understanding, and direct file analysis. While Copilot is a corporate assistant, **Gemini is a universal AI**, able to assist both professionals and casual users, content creators, educators, and developers.

Where Gemini Excels

1. Seamless Ecosystem Integration

Gemini stands out for users already embedded in Google's suite of products. If you use Gmail for communication, Calendar for scheduling, Docs and Sheets for documentation, and Drive for storage, Gemini becomes an **intelligent overlay** across your digital life.

It can:

- Summarize lengthy email threads directly in Gmail.

- Suggest edits inside Google Docs in real-time.

- Automatically generate reports using data from Sheets.

- Help plan and book travel using real-time search results.

2. Multimodal Power

With the introduction of Gemini 1.5, users gain access to **1 million tokens of context**, allowing the AI to understand, retain, and process **massive volumes of information**. You can upload a thesis, a 200-page PDF, or hours of YouTube transcripts and ask Gemini to summarize, analyze, or convert the content into a usable format — something that even GPT-4 struggles to handle in bulk.

3. Real-World Productivity Use Cases

Gemini thrives in areas such as:

- Creating structured agendas from email discussions.

- Designing content calendars for blogs and social media.

- Generating YouTube script ideas based on channel analytics.

- Providing image descriptions or alt text for accessibility.

- Helping students revise by simplifying complicated concepts.

4. Native Voice Interaction

Gemini's **voice-first approach** on Android devices, and its close link with Google Assistant, means it can operate hands-free. Set reminders, ask it to explain a topic, search files on your Drive, or create a document — all without typing a word.

Where Gemini Still Lags

Despite its power, Gemini isn't without limitations.

- **Less accessible third-party plugin ecosystem**: While ChatGPT has a rich plugin store, Gemini is more closed in its interactions with external platforms beyond the Google ecosystem.

- **Fewer community-developed tools**: OpenAI and Microsoft benefit from massive developer communities. Gemini is growing, but still trails in terms of third-party libraries, extensions, and user-generated integrations.

- **Occasional response delays with larger queries**: Due to the huge token processing capacity, Gemini might take longer when summarizing large volumes of content or analyzing extensive files.

- **Limited offline capabilities**: Unlike some versions of Copilot or

Claude, Gemini heavily relies on internet access due to its integration with live Google services.

Choosing the Right AI for Your Goals

The ideal AI tool for you depends on your workflow, ecosystem preference, and primary objectives.

You Might Prefer Gemini If:

- You're deeply integrated into Google Workspace.

- You work with multimedia files (videos, images, PDFs).

- You want hands-free mobile interaction.

- You rely on AI to manage your day-to-day tasks across email, calendar, and docs.

You Might Prefer ChatGPT If:

- You enjoy natural, creative, story-driven interactions.

- You want access to third-party plugins like Expedia, Wolfram Alpha, or Zapier.

- You're building chatbots, games, or writing fiction.

You Might Prefer Claude If:

- You need an AI that prioritizes safe, ethical dialogue.

- You're in an educational or sensitive field requiring careful phrasing.

- Transparency and principled reasoning are essential to your workflow.

You Might Prefer Microsoft Copilot If:

- You're a heavy user of Excel, Word, PowerPoint, or Outlook.

- Your team uses Microsoft Teams or SharePoint for collaboration.

- You work in a corporate or enterprise IT environment.

Using Gemini Alongside Other AIs

The good news? You don't have to choose just one. Many advanced users build a workflow combining the strengths of multiple AIs. Here's how a hybrid approach might look:

- **Start with ChatGPT** for brainstorming creative angles, generating outlines, and coming up with variations of phrasing.

- **Switch to Gemini** to format your content directly in Google Docs, integrate data from Sheets, and prepare it for publication.

- **Use Claude** to review for ethical clarity or tone-sensitivity.

- **Finish with Microsoft Copilot** if you're assembling a final business presentation or Excel report.

This AI synergy maximizes efficiency and leverages the best features of each platform.

Chapter 12

The Future of Google Gemini

The Evolution So Far

Google Gemini is more than just a rebranded version of Bard—it represents a bold shift in how Google envisions artificial intelligence shaping our digital lives. Since its launch, Gemini has grown rapidly in both functionality and intelligence. The introduction of **Gemini 1.0**, followed quickly by **Gemini 1.5 Pro**, marked a turning point in AI capability, especially with the ability to handle **1 million tokens** of context and to interact with a variety of content types—including text, images, audio, video, and documents.

But Google's ambitions for Gemini go far beyond just conversational AI or productivity support. Gemini is positioned to become the central brain of the Google ecosystem, eventually woven into Android, smart home devices, wearables, augmented reality, and beyond.

The Roadmap of Gemini's Development

From Bard to Gemini

Gemini's journey began under the Bard project, initially launched as Google's response to OpenAI's ChatGPT. While Bard laid the groundwork, it had clear limitations in context awareness, response depth, and multimodal interaction. With the rollout of Gemini, especially Gemini 1.5, Google transitioned to a more **foundational, long-context, multimodal architecture** that supports vastly more powerful capabilities.

The **Gemini AI model family** includes:

- **Gemini Nano** – Designed for on-device use (especially mobile).

- **Gemini Pro** – For general usage and integration into Google services.

- **Gemini Ultra** – Future-tier designed for more enterprise-level or extreme compute capabilities.

These versions are built to scale, so users from casual consumers to advanced developers can access the level of AI sophistication they need, without sacrificing speed, security, or personalization.

The Immediate Roadmap

Based on public developer documentation, interviews with AI leads, and updates in Google I/O and blog posts, here's what users can expect in the near-term roadmap:

1. **Full integration into Android OS** – Gemini will become the default assistant across Android devices, replacing Google Assistant in many contexts.

2. **Offline AI with Gemini Nano** –
   The ability to run Gemini on-device
   for faster, private, and reliable use,
   even without internet.

3. **Smarter Workspace Tools** –
   Expanded real-time collaboration in
   Docs, Sheets, and Gmail with
   predictive, AI-powered suggestions.

4. **Enhanced memory and
   personalization** – Gemini will
   retain user preferences, learning
   styles, and patterns to personalize
   responses further.

5. **Developer and enterprise APIs** –
   Broader access for developers to build
   apps, tools, and AI experiences

powered by Gemini.

What to Expect in Future Versions

Gemini Nano: On-Device AI Power

Gemini Nano is a miniaturized, efficient version of Gemini that runs **directly on mobile hardware**, such as Pixel smartphones. Unlike cloud-based AI, Gemini Nano offers:

- **Ultra-low latency** responses.

- **Offline functionality**, ideal for privacy or low-connectivity environments.

- **Integration with device sensors**, enabling smarter interactions using GPS, camera, microphone, and notifications.

Nano will handle tasks like summarizing text messages, suggesting auto-replies, identifying patterns in your schedule, and giving privacy-focused AI help without ever sending data to external servers. It brings the **power of generative AI** right into your pocket—no server lag, no data exposure.

As mobile chips become more powerful (e.g., Tensor G3 and beyond), the capabilities of Gemini Nano will continue to expand, making it one of the most significant breakthroughs in **on-device AI**.

Gemini in Android OS

Google has made clear its vision of integrating Gemini deeply into Android. Unlike Google Assistant, which focused on voice commands and search, Gemini will serve as a **contextual, multimodal co-pilot** that helps users do more across every app and screen.

Key features expected include:

- **Screen contextual awareness** – Gemini can read, understand, and react to the content on your screen, offering intelligent suggestions or summaries.

- **Enhanced voice commands** – Natural conversations with Gemini will enable smart task automation, like adjusting settings, replying to messages, or launching apps with intent-based logic.

- **In-app collaboration** – For instance, while composing a text in WhatsApp or crafting an Instagram caption, Gemini could suggest phrasing, emojis, hashtags, or even analyze engagement potential.

- **Multimodal task chaining** – You could show Gemini a photo, ask it to analyze it, generate a post about it, and schedule it for sharing—all in one fluid process.

Gemini will likely replace or merge with Google Assistant entirely, becoming the go-to AI for Android users globally.

AI Trends and Gemini's Place in Them

Multimodal AI Becomes Standard

The next wave of AI is multimodal—capable of understanding not just text, but also **images, video, voice, audio, code, documents**, and even real-world sensory data. Gemini is at the forefront of this transition, already enabling users to:

- Upload YouTube videos for summarization.

- Analyze images and diagrams for educational use.

- Parse PDFs and documents for insights.

- Transcribe and summarize voice recordings.

As AI models grow in context depth and modality width, Gemini is uniquely positioned to be a **universal AI engine**, able to interact across all human input types.

On-Device AI Becomes Essential

With growing privacy concerns and demand for low-latency interactions, **edge AI**—AI that runs on-device—is seeing rapid advancement. Gemini Nano is Google's solution for this, and as it improves, more AI functions will be handled locally. Expect Gemini to evolve into an **AI that lives on your phone, learns with you, and adapts to your needs**, while respecting your privacy.

Personalized and Predictive AI

Rather than being just reactive, AI is becoming **predictive** and **proactive**. Gemini will anticipate what you need before you ask. For example:

- Notifying you about an upcoming flight with your boarding pass ready.

- Summarizing your unread emails in the morning.

- Offering script suggestions when it notices you've opened your video editing app.

- Recommending meeting times based on your colleagues' and your own preferences.

This trend is central to Gemini's future—an AI that not only listens but **thinks ahead** for you.

Collaborative and Agentic AI

AI is also transitioning from a **tool** to a **collaborator**. Gemini will serve as an agent that works with you to complete tasks end-to-end. Whether it's creating a presentation, booking travel, or writing and sending follow-up emails after meetings, Gemini aims to reduce friction and manual effort in knowledge work.

In the long-term, we may see **Gemini-powered agents** that work semi-independently on your behalf—ordering supplies, responding to customer queries, conducting research, or updating spreadsheets while you focus on strategy.

How to Stay Updated and Keep Evolving with Gemini

To remain aligned with Gemini's rapid development, users should adopt a proactive mindset and tap into available resources that provide ongoing learning and insights.

1. Follow Official Channels

- **The Google Blog**: Regularly publishes updates about AI advancements, releases, and roadmap discussions.

- **Gemini's Official Page**: Offers changelogs, feature previews, and access instructions for new models.

- **Google I/O Event (Annual)**: Where Gemini updates, demos, and future directions are often unveiled.

2. Join AI and Developer Communities

Platforms like:

- **Reddit (r/GoogleGemini, r/Artificial)** – Peer insights, use cases, and feature discussions.

- **YouTube Tech Creators** – Many publish tutorials, comparison videos, and Gemini experiments.

- **Discord Groups or Substack Newsletters** – Stay ahead with beta feature leaks and early access tools.

3. Experiment with Gemini Labs

Google offers **Gemini Labs**, a sandbox environment where users can test unreleased or experimental features. Participation here gives you early access to capabilities before the general public—and helps you shape the product with feedback.

4. Upskill with Tutorials and Guides

Leverage resources such as:

- Google's own **Gemini training center** or Workspace tutorials.

- Online platforms like Coursera, Udemy, and YouTube that offer **Gemini-focused courses**.

- Blogs and eBooks that showcase real-world use cases across industries.

5. Embrace Cross-Platform Integration

Stay flexible. While Gemini will grow in power, other AI platforms like OpenAI, Anthropic, and Microsoft will also innovate. Learn to **combine tools**—Gemini for productivity, ChatGPT for brainstorming, Claude for sensitive writing, Copilot for office automation.

Staying adaptive ensures you remain ahead, no matter which AI wins the race.

A Future Built on Intelligence and Intuition

The future of Gemini is not just about making AI smarter—it's about making your life easier, your work more efficient, and your creative process more powerful. As AI evolves from a command-line interface to a seamless, intuitive collaborator, Gemini stands at the intersection of innovation, accessibility, and utility.

By embracing the capabilities today and keeping an eye on what's next, you place yourself in the driver's seat of a digital revolution. The next decade will be shaped not by who has the most data, but by who can use AI to extract the most meaning—and Gemini is designed to help you do just that.

Conclusion

As you reach the final page of this guide, you've just completed a deep and transformative journey through the world of Google Gemini. What began as a simple curiosity about a new AI tool has now evolved into a comprehensive understanding of how this technology can profoundly impact nearly every area of your personal and professional life. From enhancing productivity and creativity to supporting education, business, and daily tasks, Gemini is more than just an assistant—it's your digital thinking partner.

Key Takeaways from the Book

Throughout the chapters, we've explored not just what Gemini is, but how to practically and powerfully integrate it into your routines. You've learned how to access and navigate Gemini's features across platforms, structure effective prompts, and harness it for everything from scheduling and writing to brainstorming and research. You've seen how Gemini compares with other AI tools, its unique advantages, and even its multimodal magic—an ability to interpret and respond to images, video, and audio. We've also explored Gemini Advanced (1.5 Pro), giving you a glimpse into the higher-tier capabilities for complex, long-context tasks.

Just as importantly, you've discovered how Gemini supports responsible use in education and business, including ethical considerations and creative applications. You've seen that AI is not here to replace your thinking—but to elevate it.

Making Gemini Part of Your Digital Lifestyle

Now that you've gained this foundational and forward-looking knowledge, the next step is simple: apply it. Let Gemini become an integral extension of how you live, work, and think. Make it your creative partner when you're stuck on a blank page. Let it summarize, organize, and assist in making sense of overwhelming data or inboxes. Set up workflows that allow Gemini to handle the repetitive, so you can focus on what matters most—innovation, connection, and growth.

Explore how Gemini can complement other Google Workspace tools and even collaborate across platforms with tools like Canva, Notion, and Slack. Whether you're a content creator, entrepreneur, student, or professional, there's a version of Gemini's intelligence waiting to support your next big idea.

Encouragement for Ongoing Exploration and Mastery

The AI landscape is evolving at record speed, and what you've learned today is just the beginning. As Gemini continues to advance—especially with developments like Gemini Nano, deeper Android OS integration, and future multimodal upgrades—so should your knowledge and curiosity. Stay updated, experiment often, and don't be afraid to push the limits of what AI can do for you.

Mastery isn't about knowing every feature; it's about consistently applying the tool to solve real problems in smarter, faster, and more innovative ways. The more you interact with Gemini, the more intuitive it becomes. You'll grow more skilled in prompting, more efficient in automation, and more inspired in your work.

Let this book serve as your launchpad. The real journey starts now—where your ideas meet intelligence, your tasks meet automation, and your creativity meets unlimited possibility. Keep exploring. Keep prompting. Keep evolving.

Gemini isn't just the future. With you, it's the present—and it's powerful.

Appendix

This appendix is your practical toolkit—a quick-reference resource packed with sample prompts, shortcut commands, and trusted sources to help you continue getting the most out of Google Gemini. Whether you're refining your writing, streamlining your workflow, or exploring advanced AI interactions, these tools will empower you to act with confidence and efficiency.

Sample Prompts by Use Case

Productivity Prompts

- "Summarize the key points from this 10-page report and suggest action steps."

- "Create a weekly to-do list based on my calendar events and emails."

- "Organize these meeting notes into bullet points with clear next steps."

- "Remind me to submit the monthly sales report every 30th by 4 PM."

- "Write a professional out-of-office email that includes my return date and contact info for urgent matters."

Writing Prompts

- "Write a 500-word blog post on how AI is transforming small businesses."

- "Improve this email's tone to be more persuasive and friendly."

- "Draft a social media caption for a product launch targeting millennials."

- "Generate 5 headline options for a newsletter about remote work."

- "Convert this bullet list into a compelling promotional paragraph."

Educational Prompts

- "Summarize the causes and effects of the Industrial Revolution in under 300 words."

- "Create a quiz with 5 multiple-choice questions on the water cycle."

- "Explain quantum computing to a high school student in simple language."

- "Find and cite three credible sources for a paper on climate change."

- "Turn this dense article into key points I can use for studying."

Business Prompts

- "Generate a customer service response for a complaint about delayed shipping."

- "Write a business plan outline for a new coffee shop targeting remote workers."

- "Create a product description for an eco-friendly water bottle in an upbeat tone."

- "Summarize this market research PDF into insights and recommendations."

- "Schedule three LinkedIn posts promoting our new webinar series."

Gemini Shortcut Commands and Quick Functions

Here are useful shorthand phrases and Gemini-specific commands that help you move faster through your daily tasks:

- **"TL;DR this"** – Summarizes long content quickly.

- **"Turn this into a to-do list"** – Converts unstructured text into actionable items.

- **"Rephrase more formally/casually"** – Adjusts tone instantly.

- **"Create table from this data"** – Converts raw info into tabular format.

- **"Visualize this as a chart/graph"** – Requests graphical representations.

- **"Explain like I'm five"** – Simplifies complex topics.

- **"Add bullet points and highlight key points"** – Refines structure for clarity.

- **"Schedule this in Google Calendar"** – Initiates calendar event creation (linked setup required).

- **"Translate to [language]"** – Outputs multi-language versions.

- **"Summarize this YouTube video"** – Extracts key points from video links.

Resources to Stay Updated on Gemini and AI

To keep up with Gemini's fast-evolving features and best practices, use the following resources for trusted updates, learning, and community engagement:

Official Google Resources

- **Google AI Blog** – Announcements, research breakthroughs, and new feature insights.

- **Gemini Help Center** – Tutorials, troubleshooting, and official usage guidance.

- **Google Workspace Updates** – News on Gemini integration into Google Docs, Sheets, and Gmail.

Learning & Community Platforms

- **Reddit – r/GoogleGemini** – Real-user tips, experiences, and troubleshooting discussions.

- **Stack Overflow** – Technical questions and AI development threads.

- **[YouTube AI Creators & Reviewers]** – Search for creators sharing practical use cases, tutorials, and reviews.

- **Medium AI Articles** – Deep dives, case studies, and personal perspectives on AI usage.

Recommended Newsletters & Channels

- *"The Algorithm" by MIT Tech Review* – Curated updates on emerging AI trends.

- *"Ben's Bites"* – AI tools, updates, and news digest in daily newsletter format.

- *Gemini Labs (Unofficial YouTube)* – In-depth video guides and comparisons.

Whether you're a student, creator, entrepreneur, or everyday tech enthusiast, this appendix serves as your bridge from learning to mastery. Bookmark it. Refer to it often. And most importantly, continue exploring the full potential of Gemini as it evolves.

The power of AI is no longer a future concept—it's in your hands now.